The Story of
CAPE COD

by
Kevin Shortsleeve

Illustrated by
Elka Iwanowski

©1993 ©1996 A **CAPE COD LIFE** Including Martha's Vineyard & Nantucket Book

Special Thanks to:

Brian and Judy

Laura Reckford, Amy Preuss & Robert Ostergaard

The Woods Hole Oceanographic Institution

The Osterville Free Library

All the kind people from Historical Societies of Cape Cod and the Islands.

The Wisconsin Glacier

Design & Layout:

Amy E.V. Preuss

Jennifer Fenuccio

Jude Madden

REVISED EDITION

Library of Congress Catalog Card Number
96-084583

PRINTED IN CANADA

Dedicated to our parents,
who brought us to the Cape.

And so you are here, on the Land of Cape Cod,
Where the whalers and sailors, and hermit crabs trod.
You can see the smooth shore, with its soft sandy beach,
And the motion-filled ocean, where playful whales breach.

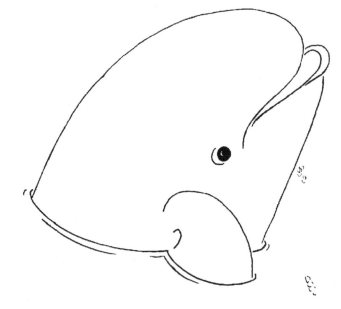

But perhaps you don't know, the tale of this land,
For the tale of Cape Cod, is as old as the sand . . .

Our story begins, when the earth was all new,
Continents forming, skies turning blue.
Where Cape Cod would be, was just smoke and steam,
With red flowing lava, forming great burning streams.
No creatures walked, no ocean flowed.
Just the sun and the moon, and the volcano's red glow.

After some years, a billion or so,
Old fossils and clues, tell us what we now know.
A great ancient ocean, covered up the Cape's earth,
With huge splashing monsters, submerged in the surf.

There wasn't much land here, in dinosaur days,
Just small swampy islands, green plants and hot haze.

By one million B.C., the monsters were done,
With the sands of time turning, a new age was begun.
An age filled with ice, and freezing degrees,
With white snowy storms, and a deep chilling breeze.

There were mile high mountains, of ice in the sky,
And slow woolly mammoths, wandering by.

But change came again, the mammoths were gone,
The big freeze was over, warm days were to dawn.
Those mountains of ice were melting away,
Moving more north, with each warmer day.
Those glaciers were heavy, they tore up the land,
Carving and shaping, with a cold heavy hand.

When the sculpting was done,
and the cold land thawed,
What was left was the land,
that we now call Cape Cod.

With islands to the south,
  a bay to the north,
An ocean to the east,
  it would be so hence forth.
This land we would know,
  as "The Arm In The Sea,"
Was born from the glacier,
  and was as it would be.

CAPE COD BAY

ATLANTIC OCEAN

CAPE COD'S SHORELINE
NOT LONG AFTER GLACIERS

CAPE COD

NANTUCKET SOUND

MARTHAS VINEYARD

NANTUCKET

Next came the people, hunters from the west,
Strong men searching shores, where fishing was best.
These were the first people, to step in the sand,
To discover the beauty, of a special new land.

They danced by their fires, and told stories of stars,
And legends of giants, building cliffs and sand bars.
The Wampanoag people, shared the land with the deer,
Season upon season, year upon year . . .

Many moons passed at peace by the sea,
Till one day, some say, in 1000 A.D.
The Vikings arrived under striped sail and oar,
The first Europeans to reach this far shore.

Leif Ericson liked the south shore of Cape Cod,
So he built several shelters of hardwood and sod.
He hunted the animals, all sizes and shapes,
And happily harvested big boatloads of grapes.
So happy was Leif in his new neighborhood,
That he named the new land, "Vinland the Good."

Then Thorfin and Thorwald sailed over to see,
This land that Leif loved on this side of the sea.
But they met up with natives and a Wampanoag chief,
Who didn't much care for Thorfin, Thorwald . . . or Leif.
Then just when old Thorfin had finally unpacked,
Both sides got angry, and both sides attacked.

So with the wind blowing East
      they packed up at dawn,
And the Redskins watched happily
      till the Yellowhairs were gone.

They could live other places,
      lands less ill-begotten,
So the secrets and treasures
      of Vinland were forgotten.

17

Six hundred years after the Vikings withdrew,
The next guest arrived, in 1602.
He'd sailed 3,000 miles, of bleak fog and cold,
This was the Englishman, Bartholomew Gosnold.
He cruised the fair shores, and sketched out a map,
He marveled at codfish, as full nets were unwrapped.
They caught quite so many, his crew found it odd,
So dubbed he, Sir Gosnold, the fair land of "Cape Cod."

He explored the whole region, from leeward to windward,
And after his daughter, he named Martha's Vineyard.
His men stayed on Cuttyhunk, so Gosnold could roam,
But one day they told him, they missed their old home.

So he sailed back to England,
    and told of the Cape,
Where the Pilgrims of England,
    sought plans for escape . . .

Eighteen years later, in the early dawn hour,
Cape Cod was spotted, from atop the "Mayflower."

They'd fled from old England, to finally be free,
They hoped for new lives, on this side of the sea.

Nearly starved from their voyage,
    in a dark desperate mood,
They sent men ashore,
    to search for fresh food.
They saw Nauset cliffs,
    and Provincetown dunes.
They met Wampanoags,
    'neath the full harvest moon.

The natives found later,
    they were missing some corn.
Their bushels were opened,
    their baskets left torn.

Angry and threatened, the natives fought back,
But no one was hurt, in the sudden attack.

So, they sailed west to Plymouth, built a fort with four walls,
A truce was declared, with good will towards all.
From the men they called Indians, many names did they get,
Like Cuttyhunk, Nantucket, Monomoy and Manomet.

The first winter was hard,
    there were many who died,
But you might be related,
    to those who survived.
After one year,
    in this new way of living,
They sat down and feasted,
    the first Thanksgiving.

Many more were to follow, a great settlers' parade.
This new population, sought a place to do trade.
Someplace strategic, for swapping and sales,
Whether trading for deerskins, or oil from whales.
The Indians told them, to trade weapons for wheat,
They must come to the place, where the two rivers meet.
So in a place called Aptucxet, in present day Bourne,
The first general store, in New England was born.

In the yesteryear ways, of the Cape's early days,
Life was quite different, from what you know today.

You could sail to each harbor,
    with glass, geese and goats,
A true trader captain,
    on your own packet boat.

You could work blowing glass,
    into white and blue jars,
Or harvest sea salt,
    on Falmouth sand bars.
You could work in a windmill,
    and harness the breeze,
Or help to pick cranberries,
    before the first Autumn freeze.

Yes, there were pirates, who spied on our shores,
Buccaneers who brought treasures, and legends and lores.
Some say Captain Kidd, just before he was caught,
Buried a treasure, in a dark secret spot.

Somewhere on the island, called Hog, it is said,
Lies the trunk of a pirate, long gone to the dead.
People have looked, yes people have searched,
But still south of Orleans, a lost treasure is perched.

Don't forget that old master, of the Seven Sea Felony,
That treasure rich pirate, by the name of Black Belamy.
He scourged the Caribbean, loaded up with his loot,
Headed north to New England, a swift escape route.
But while passing Cape Cod, and our wretched east shoals,
Black Belamy went down, with his trunks full of gold.

No one could save him, that dark stormy night,
When his ship called the "Whidah," disappeared from all sight.
She sank to the bottom, with all her doubloons,
And stayed on the bottom, for many dark moons.
But the wreck of the "Whidah," did not drift away,
And gold coins wash ashore, to this very day.

In seventeen hundred and seventy-five,
The War of Independence finally arrived.
All rebels were called, to fight tax on tea,
And the rebel cause reached, the Strong Arm In The Sea.
At Barnstable Courthouse, brave protests and yelling,
Yarmouth made bullets, the tension was swelling.

Falmouth was fired on, by huge cannon blasts,
And Cape Codders fought back, for freedom at last.

Armed British ships surrounded the Cape.
No food could come in, no man could escape.
But brave saboteurs, from Cape Cod would fight,
And sink British ships, in the dark of the night.

Then came a great day, for all rebel souls,
When a famed British ship, sank on our shoals.
Her Majesty's "Somerset," the pride of her fleet,
A terrible fate, on the Cape did she meet.
Stuck in the current, she swept into shore,
The hull ripped apart, with the green ocean's roar.
Top ranking officers, from the British Blockade,
Were captured and locked up, by a Cape Cod brigade.

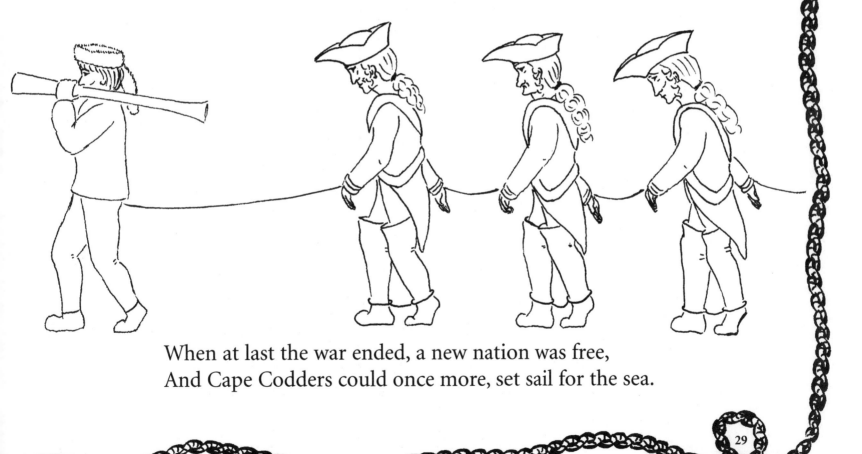

When at last the war ended, a new nation was free,
And Cape Codders could once more, set sail for the sea.

And set off they did, under broad billowed sails,
To surf the high seas, in search of the whales.
From Nantucket Island, came the great whaling fleet,
Sailing all the Earth's oceans, tugging spar upon cleat.

Cape Codders signed up,
   and shipped off to sea,
Sometimes gone for two years,
   and in some cases three.
These men sought adventure,
   far from the farm,
   Fighting sharks and monsoons,
   to them risk had a charm.
   By day they would struggle,
   and hurl the harpoon,
   At night seeking schools,
   by the light of the moon.

For 60 odd years, Cape Codders did roam,
Wishing for whales, and dreaming of home.

Herman Melville the writer, signed up with the fleet,
To learn the Earth's oceans, and gain seamen's feet.
He heard legends of whales, who sank ships with a kick,
And wrote down a story . . .

The great "Moby Dick."

East of Cape Cod, was the infamous coast,
The great ocean graveyard, of shipwrecks and ghosts.
The rip of the current, and shallow sand reef,
Led both novice and expert, to floundering grief.
From Chatham to P-Town,
       stretched the deadly wreck zone,
And to sailors all over,
       the ship's graveyard was known.

SHIPWRECKS
IN THE
"GRAVEYARD OF THE
ATLANTIC"

So up went the first lighthouse, on a tall Truro cliff,
So mariners far off, would be warned of the drift.
Beach walkers were placed, to keep lookout for ships,
Hopelessly grounded, by the Cape's tidal rips.
When trouble was spotted, in the brief nick of time,
They'd grapple the ship, with a harpoon launched line.
One by one were men rescued, ferried over the waves,

Thanking God for Cape Codders,
by whom they'd been saved.

The life saving service, of the ocean's graveyard,
Soon changed their name, to the U.S. Coast Guard.

The stage coaches rolled, along the bayside,
From Sandwich to Brewster, a dust-throwing ride.
The first summer tourist, bumped along with this load,
Travelers from Boston, on our first major road.
Inns were constructed, new folks could drop in,
From the posh Daniel Webster, to the Old Yarmouth Inn.
This road still exists, as the winding 6A,
Back then rich travelers, called it "King's Highway."

One summer traveler, who bumped along to and fro,
Was a writer from Concord, Henry David Thoreau.
He wrote of the Cape's beauty, in his thoughtful new book,
It was read by so many, that more came to look.

A later book by H. Beston, gained Cape Cod more fame,
As a quiet "time out," from the big city game.
"The Outermost House," was a tale of the beach,
About living alone, in a shack out of reach.

So began a tradition, of artists on Cape,
It was a place that inspired, to dream and escape.
A colony of artists, flooded outer Cape towns,
Painting Uncle Tim's Bridge, or a seaside sundown.

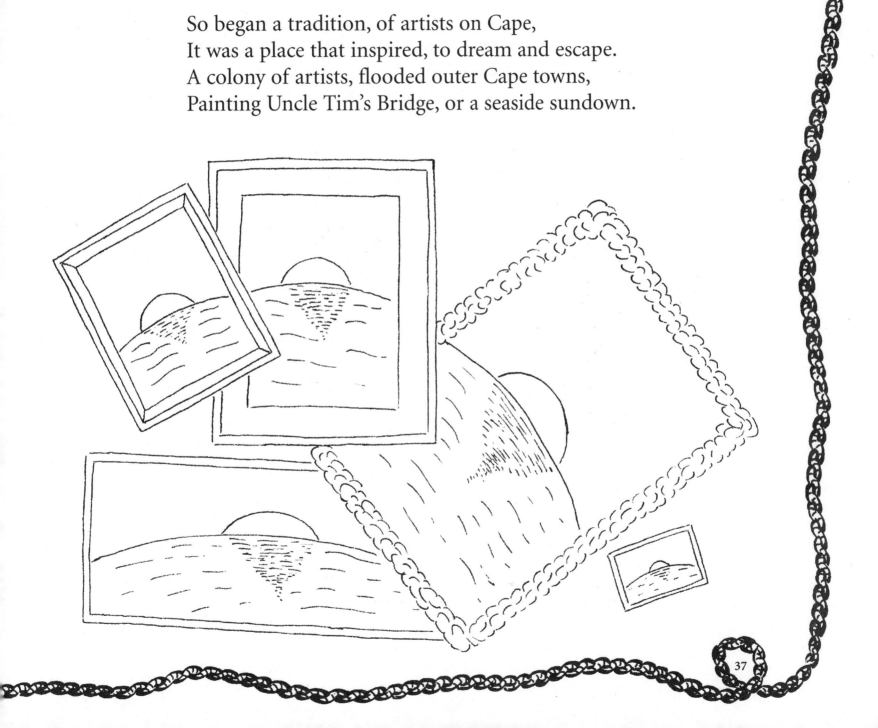

In the mid 1800's, tracks were laid down,
And the loud locomotive, hit the Cape's lucky towns.
All over Cape Cod, the steam puffed and swirled,
And Cape Cod was connected to the rest of the world.

President Cleveland, old chief of our nation,
Had for his visits, built Gray Gables Station.
Like him many more, would step in our sand,
Cape Cod was now famous, a vacationland.

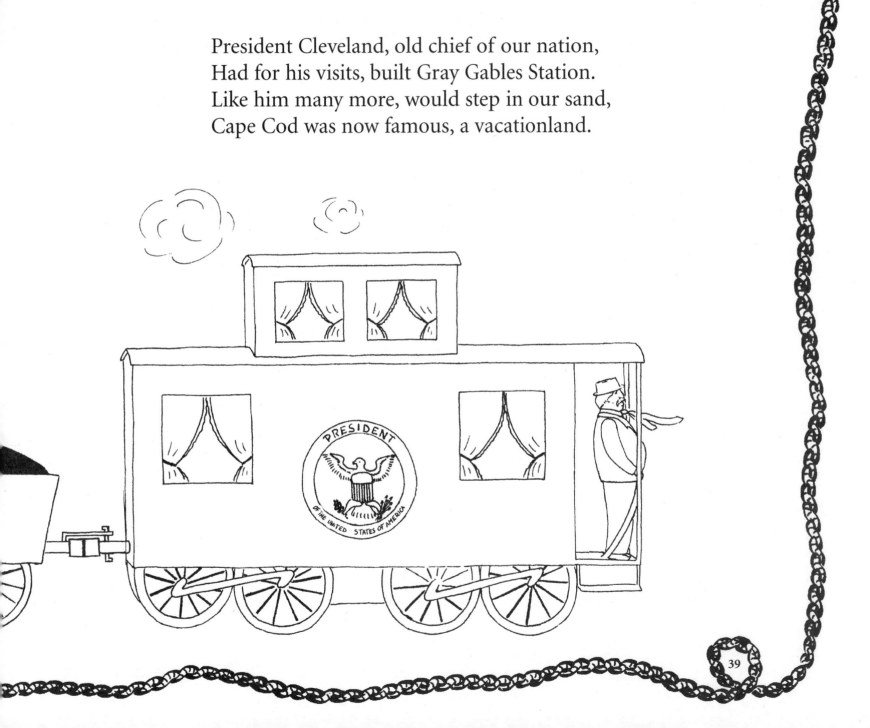

Though the locals would welcome, the warm weather comers,
There was more to Cape Cod, than what happened in summers.
Strong Yankee traditions led the worker's hard life,
The farmer, the fisherman, the innkeeper and wife.
But if one Cape profession had a good right to gloat,
Cape Codders sure knew, how to build a good boat.

Like a cat who would always, land flat on her feet,
The catboat of Crosby's was the pride of our fleet.
No matter what weather, nor how strong the breeze,
The catboats were calm, sailing upright with ease.
Any boat still afloat, when the rest would capsize,
Was a dollar well spent, to a true Yankee's eyes.

Did you know that a cable, stretched from Orleans to France,
Which was hailed as a marvelous communications advance?
It could send and take messages, both broad and precise,
America's first trans-Atlantic, transmission device!
So for the first time, you could send news away,
And it reached overseas, with just seconds delay.
All the big news of Europe came through on that line,
Shooting 3,000 miles, shoreline to shoreline.

And then came Marconi, in 1903,
Whose machine could make messages, fly over the sea.
Now faster than someone could have a note written,
The wireless message would zoom to Great Britain.

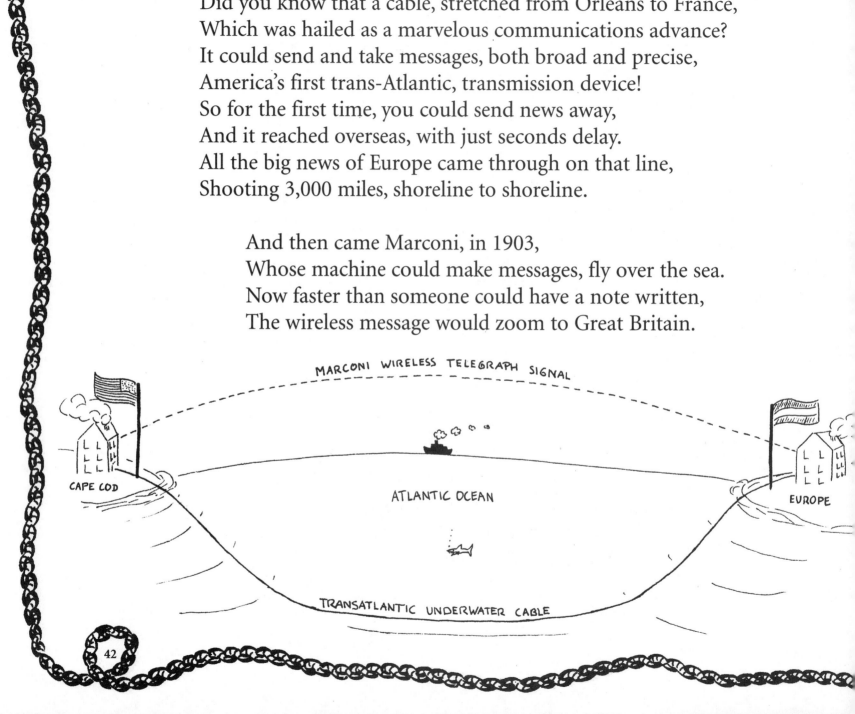

MARCONI WIRELESS TELEGRAPH SIGNAL

CAPE COD

ATLANTIC OCEAN

EUROPE

TRANSATLANTIC UNDERWATER CABLE

Did you know the one place in America attacked,
By World War One forces, was Orleans in fact?
A German sub surfaced, for a coastal showdown,
It shot up some boats, then aimed at the town.

Some think that this U-boat, from the bold German nation,
Was sent to destroy, the Orleans cable station.
But they never found out, where the station was placed,
Disguised as a house, all their bombs went to waste.

And then came the gadgets, the switches, the lights,
The gas powered motors, the high biplane flights.
The crystal set radios, with dials and knobs,
The telegraph, telephone, and other thingamabobs.

So too came the auto, which you cranked on by hand.
Then of course the first car got stuck in Cape sand.
Paved roads were needed, so paved roads were put down,
From Woods Hole to Wellfleet, and on to P-Town.

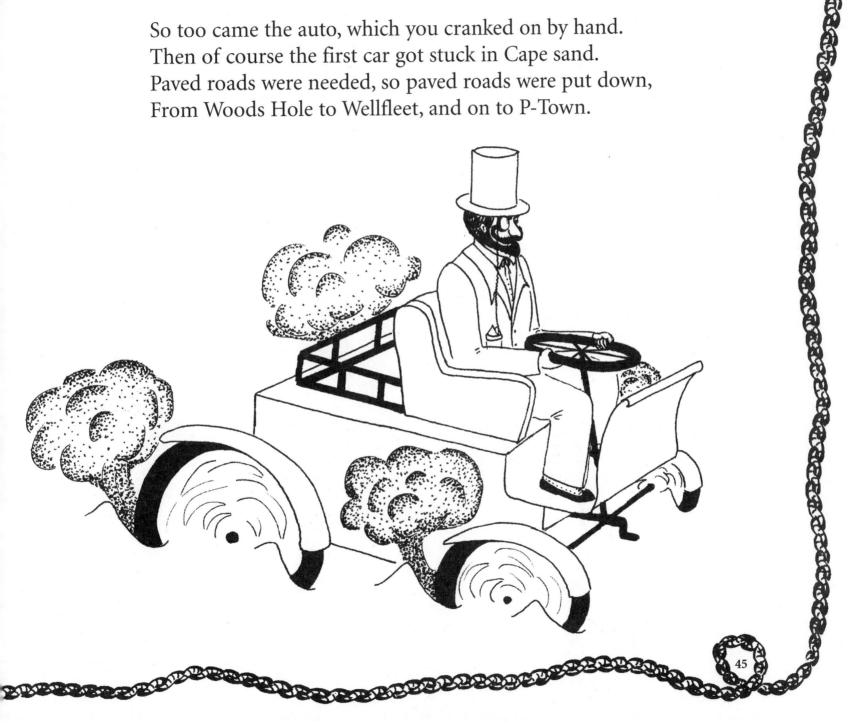

Here's something amazing, which I'm sure you'd not think,
But imagine an island, which could suddenly sink!
An island with a lighthouse, some homes and a school,
Went down in our bay, like a rock in a pool.
It's true, I'm afraid, that old Billingsgate,
Submerged like Atlantis, to its undersea fate.
It served as a pasture, and a village to live,
But 100 years, was all she could give.
No lives were lost, so suffer no fears,
The drastic erosion, took sixty odd years.

LOCATION OF
BILLINGSGATE ISLAND
BEFORE IT SANK →

Around the same time, as the island went down,
A project was started, to dig up some ground.
To take an old sea route, and shorten its shape,
To dig a long channel, straight 'cross the Cape.
It had been quite a while, since the first man complained,
Of the long, risky trip 'round the Cape's coastal lanes.

SAILING
FROM WOODS HOLE
TO PLYMOUTH

• • • AROUND THE CAPE	: 112 MILES
(((THROUGH THE CANAL	: 38 MILES

PLYMOUTH

CAPE COD
CANAL

WOODS HOLE

To sail 'round Cape Cod, added days to their trip,
And the East Coast had always, that deadly strong rip.

So they dug out a short cut, to shorten the ride,
Forty feet deep, and 500 feet wide.
Then up came the bridges, with their highway wide lanes,
Two for the autos, and one for the trains.

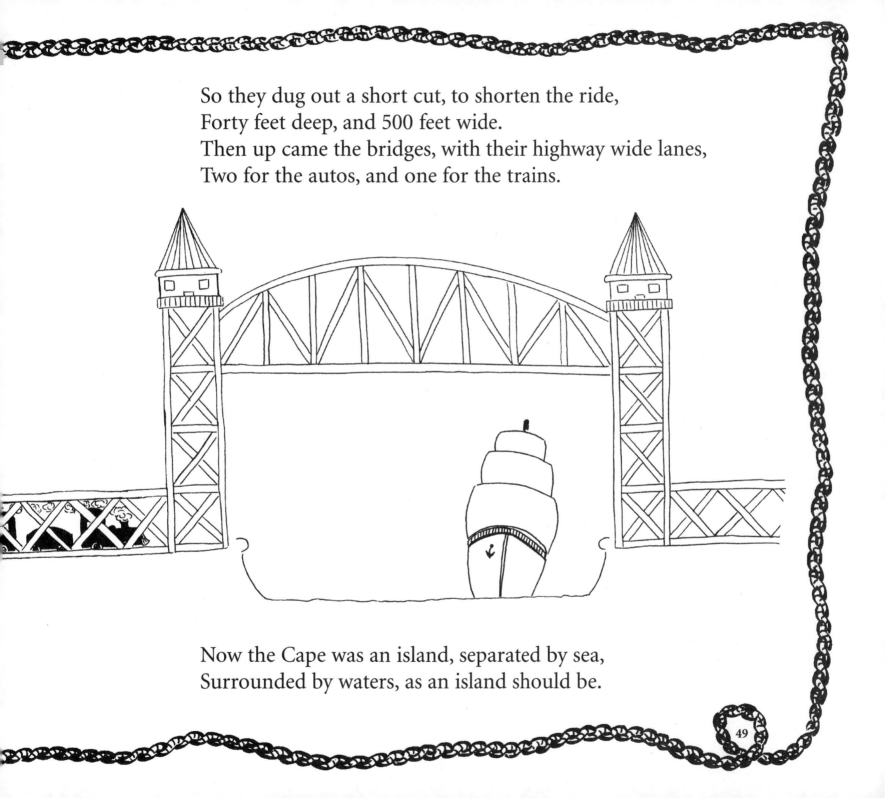

Now the Cape was an island, separated by sea,
Surrounded by waters, as an island should be.

In 1938, the bridges took a test,
A hurricane swooped down, blown in from southwest.
The bridges stayed safe, but our harbors were bashed,
Huge ships blown ashore, to the rocks they were dashed.

With winds of 100, 150, or more,
So too, struck the hurricane of 1944.
Cars flipped over, windows smashed,
Roofs ripped off, with a screaming loud crash.

And then once again in late '54,
More flooding, more flashing, more wind whipping roar.

We would have preferred it, if no more had come,
But blast down they did, in '85 and '91.

So beware of dark clouds, in the late summer sky,
Swirling 'round in confusion, with a calm sunny eye.

In 1957, a song hit the charts,
Which captured a feeling as well as our hearts.
"Old Cape Cod" by the great Patti Page,
Was sung from the radio, TV and the stage.
From the jukebox to gin joints to ballrooms with bands,
The song hit the airwaves and swept 'cross the land.

This song about sand dunes,
Romance and the sea,
Zoomed up the
Charts and hit
Number three!

Old Cape Cod
Patti Page

More famous than Patti's soft singing sound,
Is the home of one family, the Kennedy Compound.
Our 35th President, sailed here as a hobby,
With the Attorney General, his kid brother Bobby.
It seemed no solution, was too hard to reach,
For the President who solved problems, while walking the beach.

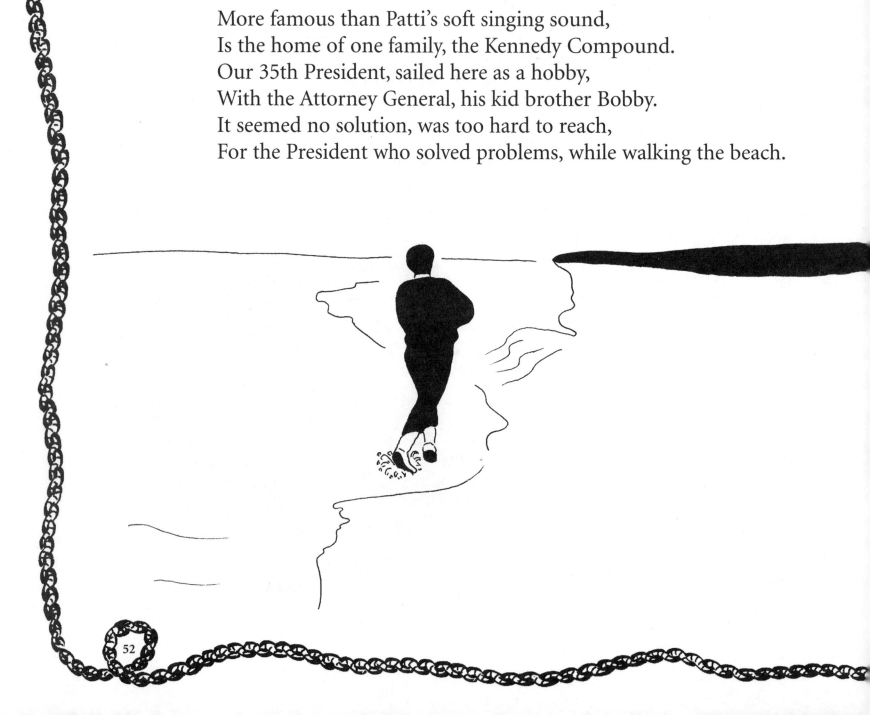

But Cape Codders remember, his deed most well done,
Was a bill which he passed, back in mid-'61.
A plan which was pushed, by the great Tip O'Neill,
When signed by the President, became a done deal.
An idea to protect, some land from our past,
A National Seashore, was preserved hard and fast.
Forty-four thousand acres of land,
Was saved for all time, from the builders' rough hand.

So now and forever, the sand dunes and trees,
May only be changed, by the rains and the breeze.

CAPE COD
NATIONAL SEASHORE
(PROTECTED LANDS)

The timing was good, since the Cape grew a lot,
For the next thirty years, folks rushed to this spot.
Houses were built, with condos and hotels,
And sign after sign, for the "best view motels."
Everyone squeezing, to shove more in less space,
Till all gift shops and mini golfs, had their own special place.
More trucks, more buses, mini malls with their mobs,
More traffic, more blacktop, more trash-throwing slobs.
On Route 28, from Bourne to Orleans,
The developers developed, vacationland scenes.

But Cape Codders fought back, and the building slowed down,
With new regulations, voted in by the towns.
Newcomers are welcome, welcome Jane, welcome Joe,
But save some green places, for our children to grow.

Like the boat builders, of a century before,
Creative Cape Codders, worked hard at their chores.
Submarine scientists, who worked in Woods Hole,
Built a small wonder, with deep diving goal.
A new fangled sub, with some undersea eyes,
And a robot for diving, of the small yellow size.
They named the thing "Alvin," then sank him below,
More than two miles down, where no man could go . . .

Diving deeper and deeper, to depths of unknown,
They found giant tube worms, the first time ever shown.

But they didn't stop there, those deep searching eyes,
One day came across, a sunken surprise . . .
In July '86, in the chill North Atlantic,
Alvin dove down, to explore the Titanic.

Today on Cape Cod, great fun can be had,
Go surfing with Mom, go fishing with Dad.
The Museum of Natural History in Brewster is nice,
With snails and rare shells, big lobsters and mice.
You could sail out of P-Town, on a whale watching trip,
Or explore the East Shore, for an old sunken ship.
There's Plimoth Plantation, and Heritage Plantation,
The Aptucxet Trade Post, old store of our nation.
Ride the smooth rails of a cool Cape Cod train,
Or look down from above, in a sightseeing plane.

And if all of these things, seem too hard to reach,
Then do like the Vikings. . .

Hang out at the beach.

Now in race the waves, under foamy white curls,
Sending splashy fun surf, for the boys and the girls.
As you play on the beach, dig your toes in the sand,
And think of the others, whose toes touched this land.
Think of the Pilgrims, the Wampanoags, the Vikings,
Think of warm summer days, and nor'easter lightings.
Consider the past, and all it has taught,
But so too must the future, be with you in thought.
Think of the sand, as it weathers away,
And shifts to new places, with each waking day.
And hope the new buildings, which cover the land,
Will respect and preserve, our history-rich sand.

THE STORY OF CAPE COD TIMELINE

Prehistory

1	70 Million B.C.	Cretaceous rock from the time of the dinosaurs.
2	8000 B.C.	Highest ground left after glacial retreat.
3	5,500 B.C.	Earliest evidence of Native Americans on Cape Cod. Archaic Period; hunter/gatherers.
	1000 B.C. to 1500 A.D.	Woodland Period; bow & arrow, farming, pottery.
4	Present Day	Wampanoag Settlement.
	550-1600	Irish and Breton fishermen explore the North Atlantic with a possible landfall at Cape Cod.
5	1001	Leif Ericson's legendary camp, at "Vinland."
	1002	Thorwald Ericson comes to Vinland.
	1010	Thorfin Karlsefni establishes temporary settlement in Vinland.

Modern European Explorers who sighted and /or explored Cape Cod prior to the Pilgrims

	1498	John Cabot for England.
	1509	Sebastian Cabot for England.
	1524	Giovanni da Verrazano for France. Names the area "Eminente Promontorio."
	1525	Estevan Gomez for Spain. Names the area "Cap de las Arenas."
6	1602	Bartholomew Gosnold for England. Maps and names "Cape Cod". Camps at Cuttyhunk. Descriptions of Gosnold's discoveries likely influenced William Shakespeare's "The Tempest."
	1605	George Waymouth for England.
	1605 & 1606	Samuel de Champlain for France. (two visits) Renames Cape Cod "Cap Blanc" (White Cape), explores Nauset area and writes a detailed account of the natives.
	1607	Captain Martin Pring for England. Begins regular trade with the natives on Martha's Vineyard.
	1609	Henry Hudson for the Dutch.
	1611	Captain Edward Harlow for England. Skirmishes with the natives and captures two.
	1614	Adriaen Block for the Dutch.
	1614	Captain John Smith scouting for Plymouth Colony. Renames Cape Cod to "Cape James," but the name doesn't stick.
	1614 & 1615	Captain Thomas Hunt, English, captures 24 natives from the Cape and Islands. Most are sold as slaves in Spain.
	1617	A French ship is wrecked on the Nauset coast. Survivors marooned in the area of Truro for three years.
	1620 (July)	Marooned French sailors picked up by Captain Thomas Dermer and carried to Virginia where Dermer dies of wounds received from the natives of Cape Cod.

The Pilgrims to the Present

7	1620 (Nov)	Pilgrims first landing site at Provincet... They explore Eastham, Wellfleet &...
8	1627	Aptucxet Trading Post established.
	1639	The towns of Sandwich, Barnstable... Yarmouth established.
	1642	The island of Martha's Vineyard receives its first European settler.
	1646	The town of Eastham established. Originally named "Nawsett."
	1659	The island of Nantucket receives its first European settlers.
	1686	The town of Falmouth established.
	1694	The town of Harwich established.
9	1699	Captain Kidd hides a treasure.
	1709	The town of Truro incorporated.
	1712	The town of Chatham incorporated.
10	1717	Black Belamy's pirate ship, the "Whidah," sinks off Wellfleet.
	1727	The town of Provincetown incorpor...
11	1760-1830	Golden age of whaling on Nantuck...
	1761	James Otis, of Barnstable, delivers... "Writs-of Assistance Speech". Th... influential speech was the first pu... cry for Independence from Engla... and also the first speech to conde... slavery in the New World.
	1763	The town of Wellfleet incorporated
12	1775-1781	The American Revolution; Cape C... surrounded by British Blockade. Falmouth, Orleans and Vineyard... Haven attacked or invaded. 177... Wreck of Her Majesty's "Somers...
13	1776-1870	Falmouth Saltworks in operation.
14	Late 1700s to Present	Crosby's boatyard in operation.
	1793	The town of Dennis incorporated.
	1797	The town of Orleans incorporated.
15	1798	First Lighthouse on Cape Cod: The Highland Light, in Truro.
16	1800s	"The King's Highway," main thoroughfare for the Cape.
17	1814	Falmouth Harbor attacked by the Br...
	1818	Steamboats begin regular service between Cape Cod and the Islan...
18	1825-1888	Sandwich Glassworks in operation
	1848	First train service reaches the Cape

	1855	"Cape Cod" by Henry David Thoreau is published.
	1870	The town of Mashpee incorporated.
	1879	Transatlantic Cable Station opens in Orleans.
	1880's	President Grover Cleveland frequents Gray Gables.
	1884	Town of Bourne incorporated.
	1893	Katharine Lee Bates of Falmouth writes "America the Beautiful."
	1898	Joshua Slocum, the first person to ever sail around the World alone, returns from his voyage and settles on Martha's Vineyard.
	1901	First automobile reaches Provincetown.
2	1903	Marconi wireless telegraph station opens in Wellfleet.
	1903	The town of Brewster incorporated.
3	1910	Pilgrim Monument erected in Provincetown.
4	1914	Cape Cod Canal opens.
5	1918	German submarine bombards Orleans.
6	1921	Cape Cod Chamber of Commerce established.
7	1928	"The Outermost House" by Henry Beston is published.
8	1929	Otis Military Reservation is established.
9	1929-Present	Home of President Kennedy and family.
10	1930	Woods Hole Oceanographic Institute established.
11	1930	The last permanent ground on Billingsgate Island washes away.
	1930's & 1940's	Hollywood's greatest actors flock to Cape Cod each summer to perform in Falmouth, Dennis and Provincetown.
12	1934	Nickerson State Park established.
	1935	Completion of the three bridges over the newly widened Cape Cod Canal.
	1936	Provincetown playwright, Eugene O'Neill wins the Noble prize for literature.
	1938	Worst hurricane in the history of Cape Cod.
	1949	Route 6, The Midcape Highway constructed.
13	1954	The Cape Cod Museum of Natural History is established.
14	1956	Plimoth Plantation opens.
	1957	"Old Cape Cod" by Patti Page hits #3 in the Billboard American Top 40.
15	1961	Cape Cod National Seashore established; Salt Pond Visitor Center.
36	1961	Cape Cod Community College established.
37	1969	Heritage Plantation opens.
38	1970	Cape Cod Mall opens.
	1979	Cape Cod Life Magazine established.
	1982	Barry Clifford locates the pirate ship "Whidah." (see 1717)
	1985	Dr. Robert Ballard, of the Woods Hole Oceanographic Institute, finds the "Titanic."
39	1990	Cape Cod Commission established for future planning and guidance.
	1991	Hurricane Bob

Numbers correspond to location on map.

PROVINCETOWN
12
23
7
TRURO
15
WELLFLEET
10
22
EASTHAM
31
3
27
34
ORLEANS
35
33
19
16
9
PLYMOUTH
32
25
24
BREWSTER
1
16
DENNIS
8
37 18
HARWICH
CHATHAM
20
SANDWICH
36 39
5
BOURNE
2 26
4
BARNSTABLE
38
28
YARMOUTH
MASHPEE
29
FALMOUTH
14
13
17
30
CUTTYHUNK
11
21
6
MARTHAS VINEYARD
NANTUCKET

Author **Kevin Shortsleeve** has written several books about Cape Cod and the Islands including *The Cape Cod Life ABC Coloring Book* and his latest work, *The Story of Martha's Vineyard*. His spiritual picture book, *God Knows*, was published last year by St. Paul Books and Media.

Illustrator **Elka Iwanowski** is responsible for the fanciful drawings that accompany the text of *The Story of Cape Cod*, *The Cape Cod Life ABC Coloring Book*, and *The Story of Martha's Vineyard*. Elka and her husband Kevin met on Cape Cod and enjoy frequent visits to the family home in Osterville.